P9-CMX-577

Anthony Fauci
Immunologist & COVID-19 Leader

by Grace Hansen

Abdo
HISTORY MAKER BIOGRAPHIES
Kids

abdobooks.com

Published by Abdo Kids, a division of ABDO, P.O. Box 398166, Minneapolis, Minnesota 55439.
Copyright © 2022 by Abdo Consulting Group, Inc. International copyrights reserved in all countries.
No part of this book may be reproduced in any form without written permission from the publisher.
Abdo Kids Jumbo™ is a trademark and logo of Abdo Kids.

Printed in the United States of America, North Mankato, Minnesota.

052021

092021

 THIS BOOK CONTAINS RECYCLED MATERIALS

Photo Credits: Alamy, iStock, Seth Poppel/Yearbook Library, Shutterstock PREMIER,
©NIAID p.13,15,17 / CC BY 2.0

Production Contributors: Teddy Borth, Jennie Forsberg, Grace Hansen
Design Contributors: Candice Keimig, Pakou Moua

Library of Congress Control Number: 2021932421
Publisher's Cataloging-in-Publication Data

Names: Hansen, Grace, author.

Title: Anthony Fauci: immunologist & COVID-19 leader / by Grace Hansen

Other title: immunologist & COVID-19 leader

Description: Minneapolis, Minnesota : Abdo Kids, 2022 | Series: History maker biographies | Includes
    online resources and index.

Identifiers: ISBN 9781098208899 (lib. bdg.) | ISBN 9781098209032 (ebook) | ISBN 9781098209100
    (Read-to-Me ebook)

Subjects: LCSH: Fauci, Anthony S., 1940---Juvenile literature. | Immunologists--Biography--Juvenile
    literature. | Political advisors--Biography--Juvenile literature. | Physicians--Biography--Juvenile
    literature.

Classification: DDC 610.8--dc23

Table of Contents

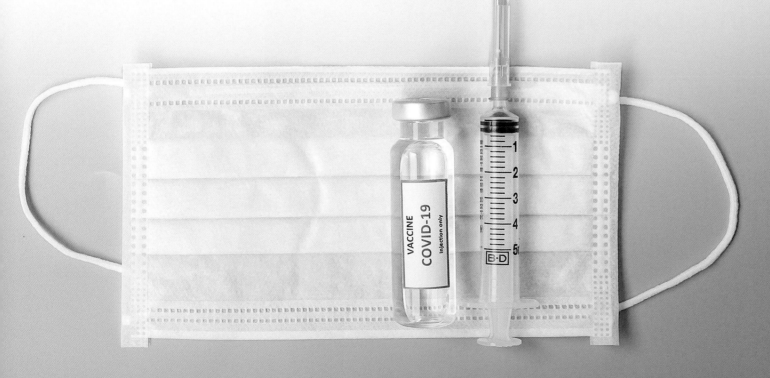

Early Years

Anthony Stephen Fauci was born on December 24, 1940. He grew up in Brooklyn, New York, where his family owned and ran a **pharmacy**.

New York

Tony's father was a pharmacist. His mother and sister helped customers. He delivered prescriptions on a bike.

Education

Tony attended Regis High School in Manhattan. He graduated in 1958. He then went to College of the Holy Cross in Massachusetts. During the summers, Tony worked on construction crews.

After college, Fauci went to Cornell University Medical College. He graduated first in his class in 1966. He then trained at New York Hospital.

Career and Achievements

Soon after, Fauci went to work at the National Institute of Allergy and Infectious Disease (NIAID). Its **mission** is to research, treat, and prevent diseases. In 1980, Fauci became chief of the new Laboratory of **Immunoregulation**.

Just four years later, Fauci was promoted to director of the NIAID. He has held this position for many years. His work has made him one of the most respected scientists in the world.

Fauci has helped every US President since Ronald Reagan. He has led the country and world through many **health crises**.

Fauci became well-known during the **COVID-19 pandemic**. In 2020, he joined the White House Coronavirus Task Force. He helped set up plans for the United States to keep the virus under control.

In January of 2021, Fauci became the chief medical advisor to the president. His experience continued to serve his country well.

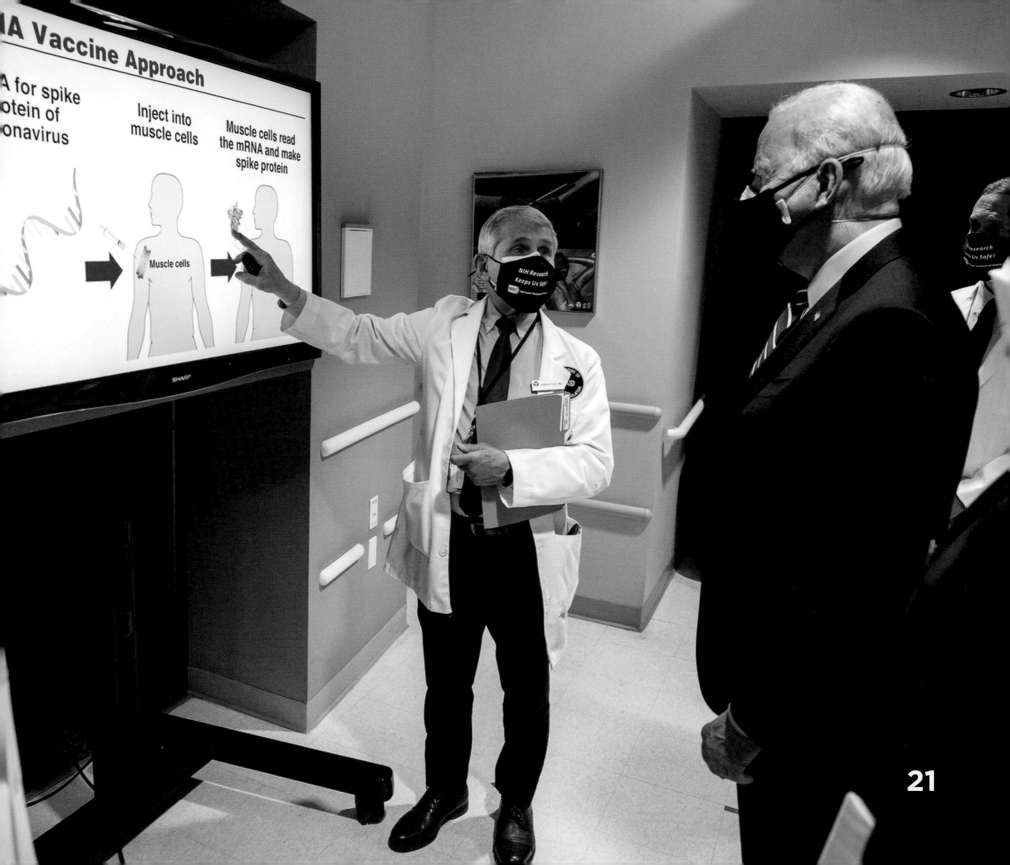

Timeline

1958
Fauci graduates from high school and attends college at Holy Cross.

1980
Fauci becomes the Chief of the new Laboratory of **Immunoregulation** at the NIAID.

2014
Fauci and the NIAID research Ebola (a deadly virus) and its treatments during an outbreak.

2021
January
Fauci begins serving as the chief medical advisor to the president.

1940
December 24
Anthony Stephen Fauci is born in New York City. He grows up in an apartment above his family's **pharmacy** in Brooklyn.

1966
Anthony graduates first in his class from Cornell Medical College. He goes on to train at the New York Hospital.

1984
Fauci becomes the director of the NIAID. His work with the institute makes him well-known in the science world.

2020
January
Fauci joins the White House Coronavirus Task Force to help lead the country through the **COVID-19 pandemic**.

Glossary

COVID-19 – short for Coronavirus Disease 2019, the illness caused by a coronavirus. Common symptoms include fever, cough, and shortness of breath and can be serious for some people.

health crisis – a health situation that affects humans in one or more areas, and generally impacts community health, loss of life, and the economy.

immunoregulation – of or relating to the regulation of the immune system, which is the bodily system that protects the body from illness-causing substances.

mission – for companies, a statement used to explain, in simple terms, its purpose or purposes for being.

pandemic – of a disease, afflicting many individuals over a large area, as a country or the world.

pharmacy – a place in which medical drugs are prepared and sold under the care of a pharmacist.

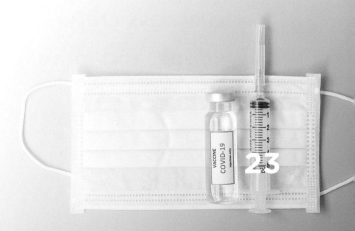

Index

Abdo Kids
ONLINE
FREE! ONLINE MULTIMEDIA RESOURCES

Visit **abdokids.com**
to access crafts, games,
videos, and more!

Use Abdo Kids code

HAK8899

or scan this QR code!